WHO WAS HENRY FORD?

BIOGRAPHY BOOKS FOR KIDS 9-12

Children's Biography Books

BABY PROFESSOR
EDUCATION KIDS

Speedy Publishing LLC

40 E. Main St. #1156

Newark, DE 19711

www.speedypublishing.com

Copyright 2017

H enry Ford was as an inventor and businessman, but is probably most famous as the founder of the Ford Motor Company. In this book, we will learn about his life and how he developed the assembly line used in manufacturing Ford vehicles.

HIS EARLY LIFE

Ford was born in Greenfield Township, Michigan on July 30, 1863 and died in Dearborn, Michigan on April 7, 1947. He grew up in Greenfield Township and his father was a farmer who had wanted his son Henry to take over the farm.

HENRY FORD

HENRY LOVES MACHINES A LOT!

However, Henry had no interest in the farm. His interests leaned more towards machines and building things. At the age of 16, he left home and moved to Detroit to become a machinist apprentice. He had two sisters and two brothers.

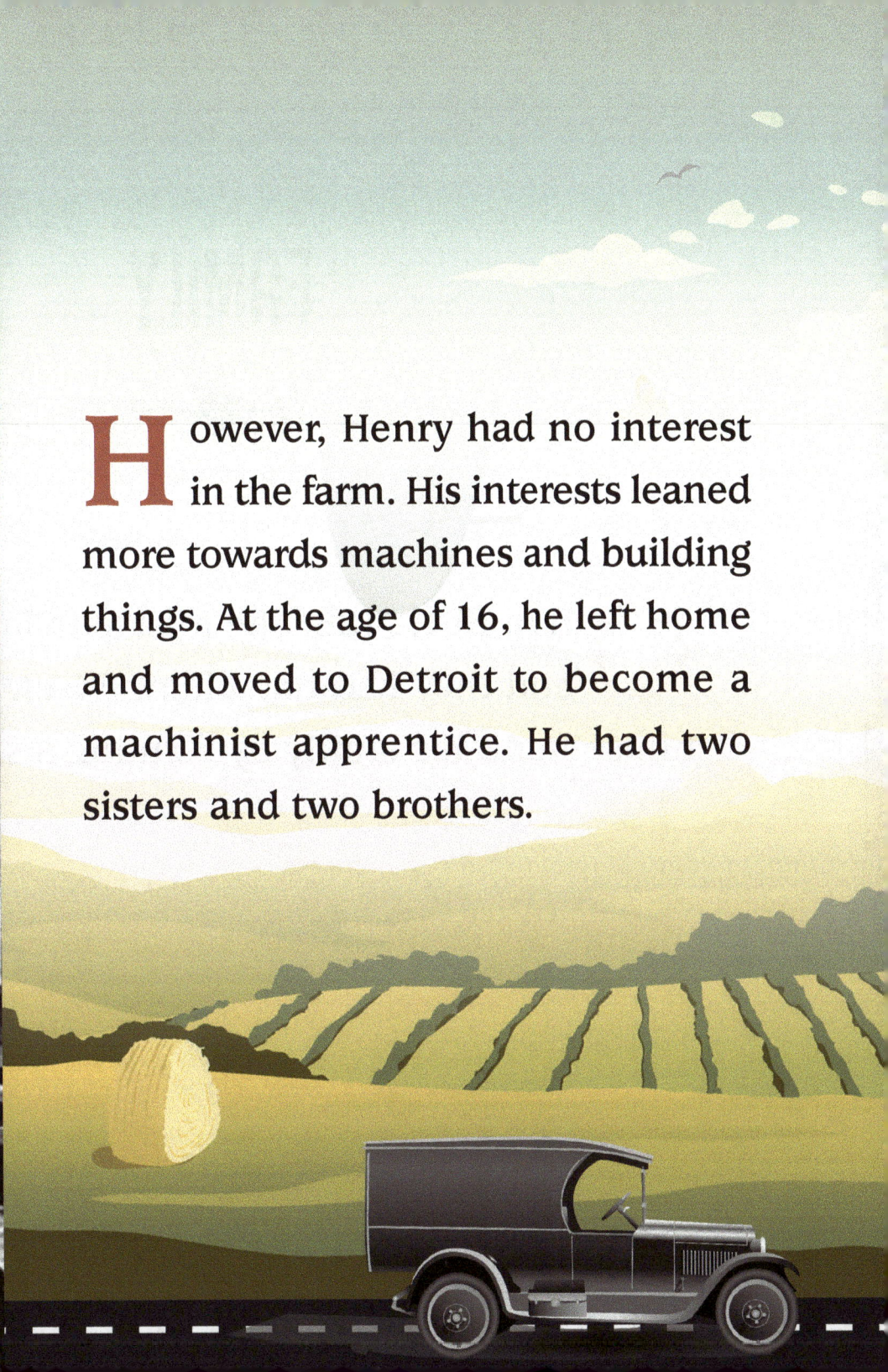

FAMILY

◆

On April 11, 1888, he married Clara Jane Bryant and they had one child, Edsel. He supported himself and his family by running a sawmill.

MR AND MRS HENRY FORD
IN HIS FIRST CAR

QUADRICYCLE

WHAT DID HE INVENT?

Quadricycle — While he worked for the Edison Illuminating Company as an engineer, Ford built his first horseless carriage that was gasoline-powered, known as the Quadricycle, behind his home in a shed.

The Model T — He established the Ford Motor Company in 1903, and rolled out the original Model T five years later. He then introduced new revolutionary mass-production methods to meet the overwhelming demand for this revolutionary vehicle, which became known as the assembly line.

FORD MODEL T 1914

AMERICAN COUPLE IN THEIR
MODEL T FORD MOBILE

The original car that he manufactured with the use of the assembly line was the Model T Ford. In many ways it was revolutionary, but primarily because of the lower cost. Its price was much cheaper than the competitive cars and it was easier to drive and repair, making it the perfect automobile for the typical middle-class American family. More than 15 million Model T autos were produced and by 1918, more than 50% of cars in America were now Model Ts.

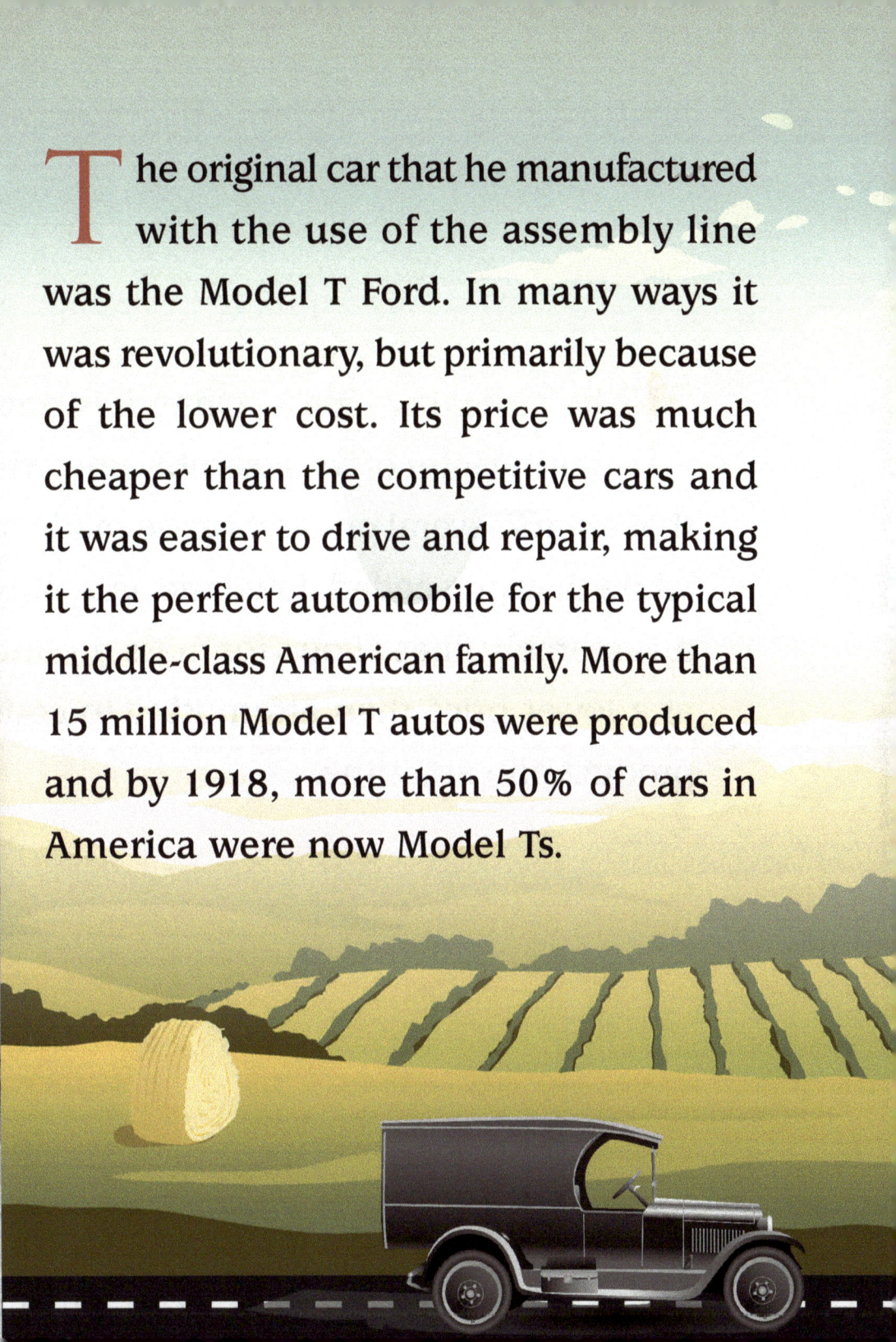

The Assembly Line — Often it is stated that Ford was the inventor of the assembly line, which is equipment that allows several products to be made one step at a time while they proceeded down the assembly line. The use of an assembly lines allows for mass production of products at a lower price than attempting to construct the entire product one at a time.

FORD ASSEMBLY LINE 1913

Ford was able to apply this idea for the automobile and perfected it for mass production of cars at a cheaper price than the current methods of production. His work in streamlining this process was one example of how powerful the assembly line would be in the mass production of other products as well.

T he Model A — The falling sales of the Model T by 1926 finally convinced him to create a new model. Ford pursued this project with tremendous technical expertise in design of the chassis, engine, and other mechanical necessities, but left the design of the body to his son. Edsel managed to prevail over the initial objections of his father about including the sliding-shift transmission.

1928 MODEL A FORD

This resulted in the success of the Ford Model A, that was introduced in December of 1927 and produced through 1931, with more than 4 million autos being built. The Ford company subsequently adopted the annual model change system which was similar to the system which was recently pioneered by General Motors, its competitors, and is still used by today's automakers).

It was not until the 1930s that he would overcome his objections to finance companies, and the Universal Credit Corporation, owned by Ford, would become a major operation for financing cars.

He did not have faith in accountants and was able to amass one of the largest fortunes throughout the world without his company ever being audited while under his administration.

FORD'S PHILOSOPHY ABOUT LABOR

Ford was the innovator of "welfare capitalism," which was designed for improvement for his workers, and in particular, for reducing the large amount of turnover that had several departments hiring as many as 300 men each year to fill 100 positions. Efficiency would result in the hiring and retention of the best workers.

THE $5 WAGE

◆

In 1914, he astonished the world offering $5 a day wage ($120 today), and this would give more than double the daily rate of most of his employees. This move proved to be greatly profitable. Other than the constant employee turnover, the best mechanics started rushing to Detroit and Ford, bringing along with them their expertise and human capital, lowering training

costs, and raising productivity. On January 5, 1914, he announced this $5 per day program, which raised the minimum daily pay rate from $2.34 to $5 for male workers that qualified.

CAR MANUFACTURING

E ven though Detroit was considered to be a high-wage city, competitors were soon forced to raise their wages or lose the best of their workers. However, Ford's policy proved that paying employees more would also enable them to be able to afford the autos they produced, which would also help the local economy.

THE REDUCED WORKWEEK

In 1926, Ford also started a new, reduced workweek. Originally decided in 1922, it was described as six 8-hour days, for a total of 48 hours per week, when it was announced in 1926, it was five 8-hour days for a 40-hour work week.

22

31

29

30

23

This decision was made to increase productivity, as the workers were now expected to put in more effort on the job and have more time for leisure, and he

also felt that good leisure time was good for his business since the workers would have more time for purchasing and consuming goods.

LABOR UNIONS

—◆—

He was against labor unions. He felt they were influenced too heavily by some of the leaders who ended up doing more harm than good for the workers, despite their good intentions. They wanted to restrict productivity as a way to foster employment. Ford felt this was self-defeating since he believed productivity was required the existence of economic prosperity.

ON STRIKE
for a decent
WAGE RAISE
to meet rising
LIVING COSTS
DRESSMAKERS'
UNION - ILGWU
AFL-CIO

ON STRIKE
for
DECENT
WAGES
DRESSMAKERS'
UNION - ILGWU
AFL-CIO

ON STR
for a dece
WAGE RAIS
to meet rising
LIVING COSTS
DRESSMAKERS'
UNION -

DRINK
Coca-Cola
ICE C

DRESSMAKERS' UNION STRIKE

The Ford Motor Company was the final Detroit automaker to acknowledge the UAW (United Auto Workers) union. In April of 1941, a sit-down strike by the union closed the River Rouge Plant. Henry Ford became distraught and threatened to destroy the company rather than to cooperate.

However, his wife advised him that she would leave him if he decided to proceed with destroying the business.

She felt that it wasn't worth the chaos that it might create. He complied with the ultimatum of his wife and, in retrospect, actually agreed with her.

FORD MOTOR CORP–UAW
AGREEMENT, 200

The Ford Motor Company, overnight, went from being the most diligent holdout among the automakers to being one with the best UAW contract terms. In June of 1941, the contract was then signed.

POLITICS AND WAR

O ver the years, his political views had earned him widespread criticism, starting with his campaign against the U.S. involvement in World War I. In 1918, he failed in a bid for a U.S. Senate seat, losing narrowly in a campaign that was marked by the personal attacks of his opponent.

When the United States proceeded to enter the war, Ford advised his company to build a new factory near Detroit, at Willow Run.

In the spring of 1942, they broke ground at Willow Run, and in October of 1942, the first B-24 was produced.

It was the biggest assembly line in the world at this time, at 3,500,000 square feet. In 1944, at its peak, this plant could produce 650 B-24s each month, and by 1945, the company had produced 9,000 B-24s at the Willow Run plant, which was half of the total 18,000 B-24s that were produced during the war.

WILLOW RUN PLANT

HENRY FORD HOSPITAL

HENRY FORD'S MENTAL COLLAPSE

In 1943, when Henry's son died prematurely, he resumed some control over the company, but he suffered strokes late in the 1930s which left him more and more debilitated, and his mental ability also started fading.

He was becoming more and more sidelined and decisions were now made by others, but in his name. The company was now being controlled by a few senior executives that were under the leadership of Charles Sorenson, production executive and an important executive at the company and Harry Bennett, who was the chief over Ford's Service Unit, which was the force that Ford used to spy on, and discipline, the employees.

H e became jealous of Sorenson's publicity and in 1944, forced him out. His incompetence led to talks in Washington regarding how to restore the company, whether it was by wartime government fiat, or by instigating some type of coup among the directors and executives.

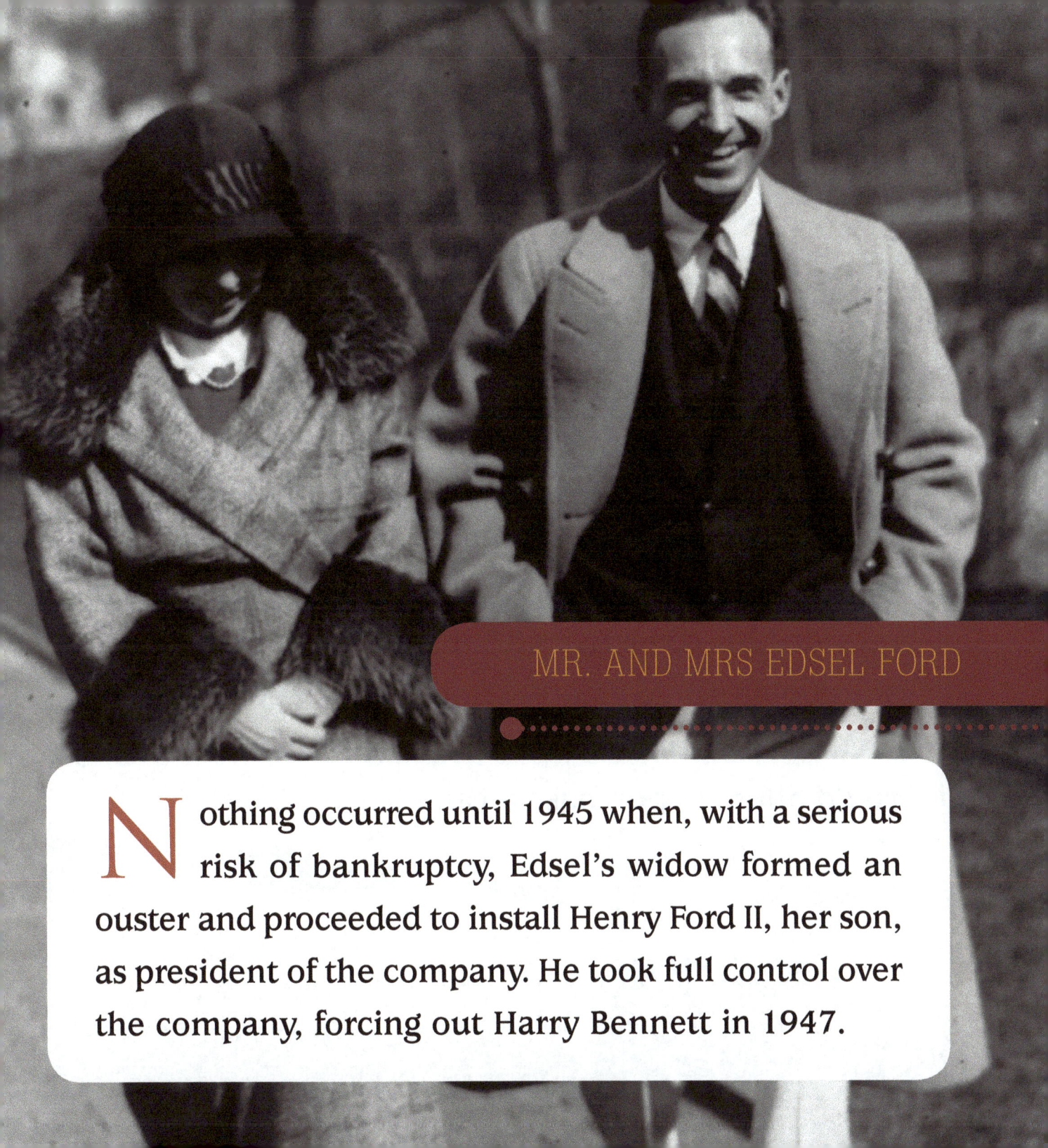

Nothing occurred until 1945 when, with a serious risk of bankruptcy, Edsel's widow formed an ouster and proceeded to install Henry Ford II, her son, as president of the company. He took full control over the company, forcing out Harry Bennett in 1947.

THE FORD MOTOR COMPANY

F ord remains of the biggest producers of cars throughout the world and includes such brands as Ford, Mercury, Lincoln, Mazda, Volvo, and the Land Rover. He was a manufacturing pioneer in using the assembly line to manufacture these cars. This provided his company with the ability to manufacture automobiles on a greater scale at a cheaper price. This was the first time that the average American family could afford to purchase a car.

FORD OAKVILLE ASSEMBLY

Henry Ford was an intelligent man that knew what he wanted to do with his life and became very successful. The next time you see a car moving down the road, think about how long it would take to build it if he had not created the assembly line.

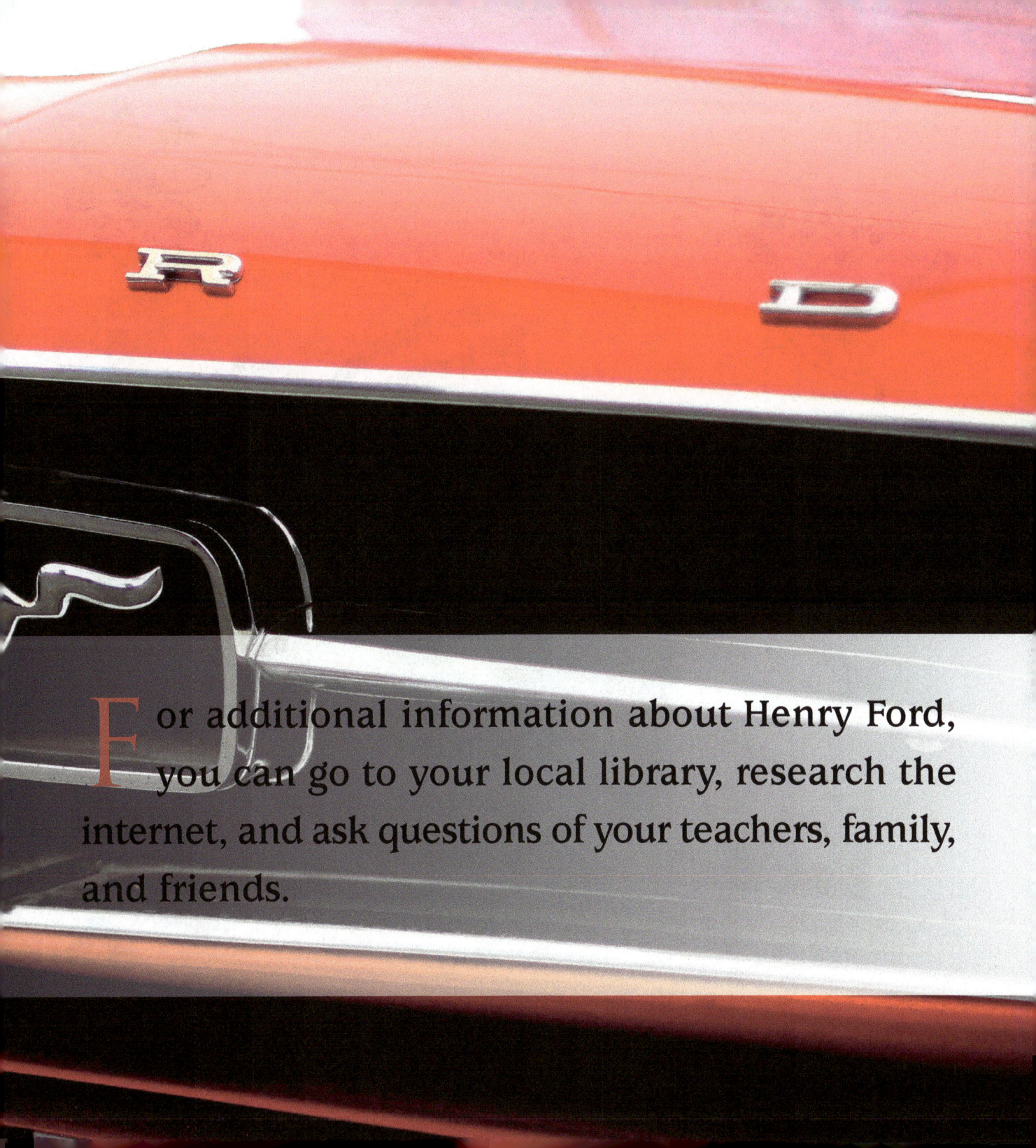

For additional information about Henry Ford, you can go to your local library, research the internet, and ask questions of your teachers, family, and friends.

Visit

BABY PROFESSOR
EDUCATION KIDS

www.BabyProfessorBooks.com

to download Free Baby Professor eBooks
and view our catalog of new and exciting
Children's Books

9 798869 413758